The
Aaronic
Priesthood

The
Aaronic
Priesthood

Seven principles that will make this power
a key part of your daily life

by
Chad Daybell

Illustrated by Rhett E. Murray

CFI

Springville, Utah

ISBN: 1-55517-717-4
e.3

Published by CFI
An imprint of Cedar Fort Inc.
www.cedarfort.com
Distributed by:

Cover design by Nicole Cunningham
Cover design © 2004 by Lyle Mortimer
Inside illustrations © Rhett E. Murray
Used by permission of the artist
Printed in the United States of America
10 9 8 7 6 5 4 3 2 1
Printed on acid-free paper

Library of Congress Cataloging-in-Publication Data

Daybell, Chad G., 1968-
    The Aaronic Priesthood : seven principles that will make this power a key part of your daily life / by Chad Daybell ; illustrated by Rhett E. Murray.
            p. cm.
Contents: Authority -- Action -- Reverence -- Obedience -- Nobility -- Integrity -- Covenants.
Includes bibliographical references.
    ISBN   1-55517-717-4 (pbk. : alk. paper)
    1. Aaronic Priesthood (Mormon Church)--Juvenile literature. 2. Church of Jesus Christ of Latter-Day Saints--Doctrines--Juvenile literature. 3. Mormon Church--Doctrines--Juvenile literature. I. Title.

BX8659.5 .D39 2003
                        2003020156

Dedicated to my sons

Garth, Seth and Mark

Table of Contents

Chapter One

Authority

Action
Reverence
Obedience
Nobility
Integrity
Covenants

Congratulations! As an Aaronic Priesthood holder, you are part of a great team that is growing each day and is sweeping the world. The gospel of Jesus Christ has been restored, along with Heavenly Father's priesthood power—the authority to act in His name. If you live righteously, you will hold this power throughout eternity.

Many men in the world hold important positions of power, but their power is only temporary. A judge has the authority to sentence a criminal to prison, but once he retires, his power is gone. Similarly, a country's president has the power to sign new laws into effect, but those laws can be changed once his term in office ends. Only those people who hold the priesthood have the power to act in the name of the Savior Jesus Christ. Through his servants, He has entrusted you with the power to act in his name.

The priesthood is restored

May 15th is a special day. On that day in 1829, a resurrected man named John the Baptist restored the Aaronic Priesthood to the earth. He placed his hands upon the heads of Joseph Smith and Oliver Cowdery, then spoke these words: "Upon you my fellow servants, in the name of Messiah I confer the Priesthood of Aaron, which holds the keys of the ministering of angels, and of the gospel of repentance, and of baptism by immersion for the remission of sins; and this shall never be taken again from the earth, until the sons of Levi do offer again an offering unto the Lord in righteousness." (D&C 13:1)

President Gordon B. Hinckley spoke of this event. He said, "Joseph Smith was then twenty-three years of age. Oliver Cowdery was about the same. They were young men, and I thought when I was ordained a deacon what a wonderful thing it was that John the Baptist, who was a great man in the New Testament and who lived nearly two thousand years earlier, had come as a resurrected being and that he should address Joseph and Oliver as 'my fellow servants.'

"Even though he came as a servant of God and acted under the direction of Peter, James, and John, he did not place himself above Joseph and Oliver. He put them on his same level when he addressed them as 'my fellow servants.' If they were his fellow servants, then perhaps I, as a twelve-year-old boy, could also be his fellow servant."

President Hinckley added that John the Baptist "spoke in the name of Messiah, or, as we would say it, 'in the name of Jesus Christ.' He set the pattern, and since then, the ordinances which we perform are administered in the name of Jesus Christ. This is something we should never forget, and never overlook, for in the exercise of our priesthood, we are acting in behalf of God our Eternal Father and Jesus Christ, His Son."[1]

The proper authority

As an Aaronic Priesthood holder, you have been ordained by someone who holds the authority from God. Joseph Smith and Oliver Cowdery later ordained other men to the Aaronic Priesthood, and it has been passed down through the years to righteous men and young men, including yourself.

You can receive the priesthood only from one who has the authority and "it is known to the church that he has authority." (D&C 42:11)

It is important to remember that the priesthood wasn't handed to you like a diploma or sent to you in a letter. It comes only by proper ordination. An authorized holder of the priesthood must place his hands upon your head and ordain you.

The priesthood is very precious to the Lord. He is very careful about how it is conferred, and by whom. It is never done in secret, and the ordination is recorded in the records of the Church.

In the scriptures, we learn that this authority is called "the Priesthood of Aaron, because it was conferred upon Aaron and his seed, throughout all their generations." (D&C 107:13)

The Aaronic Priesthood goes by other names as well. It is sometimes called the lesser priesthood. "Why it is called the lesser priesthood is because it is an appendage to the greater, or the Melchizedek Priesthood, and has power in administering outward ordinances." (D&C 107:14) The fact that it is called the lesser priesthood does not diminish at all the importance of the Aaronic Priesthood.

The Aaronic Priesthood is also referred to as the "preparatory priesthood." This, too, is a proper title because the Aaronic Priesthood prepares young men to hold the higher priesthood, to serve missions, and to take part in temple ordinances and celestial marriage.

Who was Aaron?

Aaron is a name we've heard many times, but what did this man do to deserve the honor of having this priesthood named after him?

Aaron lived many centuries ago. When he was a young man, he didn't expect to be remembered for much of anything. You see, he and his family were Hebrew slaves in the land of Egypt. Aaron's early life was spent making bricks out of straw and mud that could be used to build the great Egyptian buildings.

So while Aaron's early years were pretty boring, he had a unique younger brother who would change the history of the world—Moses.

When Moses was a baby, the king of Egypt, known as Pharaoh, ordered that all newborn boys should be killed. (Aaron was safe because he was about three years old at the time.)

Instead of letting Moses be killed, his mother sent him floating down the Nile River in a basket. Moses was discovered by Pharaoh's daughter. She adopted him, and he became an Egyptian prince. Within a few years, he moved up the ranks and was in line to be the next king of Egypt.

In those years, Moses and Aaron probably didn't know each other, but you can be certain that Aaron knew Moses' true identity and paid attention to what his younger brother was doing.

Then when Moses was forty years old, he wanted to learn more about his actual family. Moses visited Aaron and the rest of the family in the slave camp. While Moses was there, he saw an Egyptian mistreat a Hebrew slave. Moses fought with the Egyptian and accidentally killed him.

This incident caused Moses to quickly lose favor with the Egyptians, who had never forgotten he was actually a Hebrew. He immediately went from being one of Pharaoh's favorite people to becoming the No. 1 guy on Egypt's "Most Wanted List." Egyptian soldiers were told to hunt for Moses and kill him on the spot. His only choice was to leave Egypt.

Moses miraculously crossed the desert and met a righteous family in the land of Midian. Moses received the priesthood there and stayed hidden from the Egyptians. During the next forty years he became a humble shepherd, got married and raised a family. But the Lord still had big plans for Moses, and that's where Aaron comes back into the picture.

When Moses suddenly disappeared into the desert, his family in Egypt had no idea where their famous relative had gone. For forty years no one heard from Moses. Then one day the voice of the Lord came to Aaron and told him where to find his brother. The scriptures say, "And the Lord said unto Aaron, Go into the wilderness to meet Moses. And he went, and he met him in the mount of God, and kissed him." (Exodus 4:27)

Imagine if you hadn't seen your brother for forty years! It's hard enough waiting for your brother to return after a two-year mission, right? Well, it was a great reunion, and these two became inseparable.

After Moses and Aaron finished with all the typical back-slapping and catching up on the past forty years, the Lord didn't waste time in calling Moses to be a prophet.

However, Moses objected. He didn't feel up to the task. He told the Lord he didn't speak very well and sometimes stuttered. Moses felt his speech problems should disqualify him from being a prophet.

The Lord didn't accept his excuse, though. Instead, he told Moses that Aaron should be his voice. So Aaron became Moses' trusted assistant.

You can compare the relationship these brothers had to the close friendship shared by Hyrum and Joseph Smith. In both cases, the younger brother was called to be the prophet, but both Moses and Joseph depended on a wise and faithful older brother to help complete the work of the Lord.

A challenging task

Once Moses accepted his calling as a prophet, the Lord gave these brothers their first assignment. The Lord asked Moses and Aaron to return to Egypt, then to march into Pharaoh's court and tell him to free their relatives, the Hebrew slaves. Simple enough, right?

Well, Moses and Aaron chose to obey the Lord, but first they visited their relatives. Word spread quickly that Aaron had brought Moses home. You can imagine the excitement that must have surged through the slave camp when everyone heard about the brothers' assignment from the Lord. These men were going to lead them all to freedom!

Moses and Aaron soon headed off to see Pharaoh, and as they stood before him, they got straight to the point. They told Pharaoh, "Thus saith the Lord God of Israel, Let my people go." (Exodus 5:1)

Not surprisingly, Pharaoh didn't take them too

seriously. He probably laughed as he sent them on their way. But they returned three days later, and a slightly annoyed Pharaoh asked them to show him a sign that they were sent by the Lord.

Aaron responded by throwing Moses' walking stick onto the floor, and through the power of the priesthood it became a large snake!

However, Pharaoh had some magicians. They came into the room and performed some illusions. Soon there were several other snakes slithering on the floor. Pharaoh probably smirked a little, but then an interesting thing happened. Aaron's snake began devouring all the magicians' snakes! Rather than be impressed, this made Pharaoh angry, and he had his guards kick the brothers out again.

The Lord was getting tired of Pharaoh's disbelief, and now He commanded Moses to release ten plagues on the Egyptians, such as turning their water supply into blood, then sending frogs, lice, and flies. The final plague was the death of each firstborn Egyptian son. After that, the Egyptians were eager for the Israelites to leave, fearing they might all be killed.

In the following weeks Aaron helped Moses lead the Israelites out of Egypt, and he helped to teach them the gospel of Jesus Christ.

Aaron saw the Lord

A major highlight of Aaron's life came when he was allowed to actually see the Lord! Moses led

9

Aaron and some other men partway up Mount Sinai. The scriptures say, "And they saw the God of Israel: and there was under his feet as it were a paved work of sapphire stone, and as it were the body of heaven in his clearness." (Exodus 24:10) What a wonderful event that must have been!

Aaron's greatest responsibility in later years came when he and Moses were commanded to construct a tabernacle, which was like a portable temple. Once it was completed, Aaron received a special calling. He was named the High Priest, and he and his sons were given the responsibility to perform sacred rituals in the tabernacle. Aaron's sons were ordained to the lesser priesthood and were called "priests." They administered the outward ordinances of the gospel. In honor of Aaron's position as High Priest, this priesthood came to be known as the Aaronic Priesthood. In addition to the office of priest, it also included the offices of teacher and deacon.

One scholar writes that the sons of Aaron were "assigned to preach, teach, exhort, visit the people, detect evil, eliminate quarreling, and encourage attendance at Sabbath services." [2]

That sounds very similar to what Aaronic Priesthood holders are commanded to do today in Section 20 of the Doctrine and Covenants.

When Aaron was 123 years old, the Lord decided he had served long enough. The Lord told Moses to go with Aaron up into the mountain where "Aaron shall be gathered unto his people, and shall die there." (Numbers 20:26)

That's what happened, and when Moses returned and told the people Aaron had died, the entire house of Israel mourned his death for thirty days.

So that is your heritage as an Aaronic Priesthood holder.

The apostles understand its power

When I was a deacon in the early 1980s, the young men in my ward would travel from our small town to the Tabernacle on Temple Square to attend the Priesthood Session of General Conference.

On our first visit, we were seated up in the balcony, and we watched the people down on the front row get to meet the General Authorities.

We were a little envious, but that became our new goal. We decided that in six months we would be on the front row. We discovered that to do so we had to get in line several hours early outside the Tabernacle, but we did it, and it was worth it.

First of all, we happily found out that the front row was the only cushioned row. Everyone else had to sit on those hard wooden benches. The best part of all, though, was the chance to shake hands with many of the General Authorities.

Before the Priesthood Session began, several of the General Authorities came down into the audience and shook hands with the young men. Many people surrounded leaders such as Bruce R. McConkie and Paul H. Dunn. However, one apostle stood nearby, hardly noticed by the crowd. Thankfully, I had studied my chart of General Authorities in the *Ensign* during those long hours in line. I stepped toward him, extended my hand, and said, "Elder Hunter, how are you?"

He smiled warmly and replied, "I feel wonderful!" He asked my name, and I stammered a little, feeling excited to be talking to an apostle. Finally I blurted out my name and added, "Sorry, I'm a little nervous."

He smiled again. "I'm a little bit nervous myself," he said. "I have to speak in Conference tomorrow morning."

I thought that was interesting. I didn't realize General Authorities got nervous. Then he patted me on the shoulder and said, "Chad, thank you for coming tonight. Is your father here?" I said yes, and pointed to Dad a few feet away.

Elder Hunter said, "Nothing makes me happier than seeing a father and son exercising their priesthood."

The time had come to start the meeting, and we headed back to our seats—Elder Hunter to his padded chair on the stand, and me to my padded bench. Our conversation had created a glow inside me, and I felt honored to hold the priesthood.

Few people could have been more pleased than I was twelve years later when I was able to raise my hand along with the rest of the Church members and sustain him—President Howard W. Hunter—as the fourteenth president of the Church.

Elder Boyd K. Packer even commented on such events during a General Conference talk later that year. He said, "I always come to the Tabernacle early for priesthood meeting in order to shake hands with the deacons, teachers, and priests. I have to sift through a lot of elders, seventies, and high priests to find them, but it's well worth it to meet the Aaronic Priesthood. We who hold the higher priesthood salute you, our brethren of the Aaronic Priesthood."3

It is comforting to know that the apostles hold Aaronic Priesthood bearers in such high regard.

Unseen—but very real

President Packer made other important comments about the Aaronic Priesthood during that General Conference session. He said, "I want to tell you about the unseen power of the Aaronic Priesthood. A boy of twelve is old enough to learn about it. As you mature you should become very familiar with this guiding, protecting power.

"Some think that unless a power is visible it cannot be real. I think I can convince you otherwise. Do you remember when you foolishly put your finger in that light socket? While you did not see exactly what happened, surely you felt it!"

Elder Packer then added, "No one has ever seen

electricity, not even a scientist with the finest instruments. However, like you, they have felt it. And we can see the results of it. We can measure it, control it, and produce light, and heat, and power. No one questions that it is real simply because he cannot see it. Although you cannot see the power of the priesthood, you can *feel* it, and you can see the results of it. The priesthood can be a guiding and protecting power in your life."4

President Woodruff's valiant service

Aaronic Priesthood holders can use this power to bless many lives. After President Wilford Woodruff joined the Church, he desired to serve a mission.

"I was but a teacher," he wrote, "and it is not a teacher's office to go abroad and preach. I dared not tell any of the authorities of the Church that I wanted to preach, lest they might think I was seeking for an office."5

He prayed to the Lord, and without sharing his desire to anyone else, he was ordained a priest and sent on a mission to the Arkansas Territory.

He and his companion struggled through a hundred miles of alligator-infested swamps. They were constantly wet, muddy, and tired. Brother Woodruff developed a sharp pain in his knee and could go no further. His companion finally left Brother Woodruff sitting on a log, then quit his mission and headed home to his family.

Brother Woodruff wasn't ready to give up yet, though. He knelt down in the mud and prayed for help. He was healed and continued his mission alone.

Three days later he arrived in Memphis, Tennessee, weary, hungry, and still very muddy. He went to the largest inn and asked for something to eat and for a place to sleep, although he didn't have any money.

When the innkeeper found out that Brother Woodruff was a preacher, he laughed and decided to have some fun with him. He offered Brother Woodruff a meal if he would preach to his friends.

A large audience of the rich and fashionable people of Memphis gathered and were quite amused by this mud-stained missionary.

Nobody in the crowd would sing or pray, so Brother Woodruff did both. He knelt before them and begged the Lord to give him His Spirit, and the Spirit came! Brother Woodruff preached with great power. When he was finished, no one laughed at this humble holder of the Aaronic Priesthood. Thereafter they treated him with great kindness.[6]

President Woodruff was under the guiding, protecting power of the Aaronic Priesthood. The same power can be with you as well.

Every bishop, stake president, apostle and prophet began their priesthood duties as a member of the Aaronic Priesthood. Elder Packer said, "A few of you who now sit there as deacons, teachers, and priests will one day sit here as apostles and prophets and will preside over the Church. *You must be prepared.*" 7

Elder LeGrand Richards, who was Presiding Bishop for fourteen years and an apostle for many more, often said, "I'm just a grown-up deacon."

Think about it! The priesthood is yours forever unless you disqualify yourself through sin or by failing to exercise your priesthood.

Treasure it.

Chapter Two

Authority

Action

Reverence
Obedience
Nobility
Integrity
Covenants

We often talk about *exercising* our priesthood power. In some respects, the priesthood is like our muscles. If we don't use our muscles regularly, they might not perform properly when needed. The same principle applies to our priesthood.

I have always loved to play baseball, and I would play each summer on one of the city teams. One game I got a base hit and after my teammate also got a hit, I found myself standing on third base. I took a few steps off the bag, then on the next pitch, the catcher missed the ball and it rolled all the way to the backstop.

As the catcher scrambled after the ball, I raced home. He now had the ball, and it looked like it was going to be a close play, so I made an awkward slide to avoid his tag. Safe!

Then I rolled over, and saw blood soaking through my uniform. I had somehow slashed my left knee on home plate. I bent my knee to get a closer look, and was horrified to watch that gash split completely across my kneecap, all the way to the bone. My dad rushed me to the hospital, where it took eighty stitches to close the injury. My season was over.

I quickly learned that I was in for a long summer on the couch. Although I hadn't broken a bone, the doctor put my leg in a cast so I couldn't bend my knee. It was the only way the skin would heal.

Just before school started—nearly two months later—the doctor finally took the cast off my leg. It was a little frightening to compare my legs. In those two months, my left leg had seemingly shrunk and my leg muscles weren't too eager to work. It took a while to get them back into shape.

The duties of the Aaronic Priesthood are designed to keep you in top spiritual shape. By passing the sacrament, attending your priesthood quorum meetings, collecting fast offerings, and going home teaching, you build the spiritual muscles that will make you a great missionary and a worthy husband and father.

I only had my leg immobilized for two months. Imagine if I didn't use that leg for seven years — from age 12 to 19. Would my leg be at full-strength when it was time to go on a mission? Of course not, and neither would my spirit if I didn't learn to exercise my priesthood during those years.

Steve Young stood strong in adversity

You have likely heard of Steve Young, a former BYU football quarterback who would later lead the San Francisco 49ers to a Super Bowl victory. He was also twice named the Most Valuable Player of the NFL and has helped build the reputation of the Church through his example. But his rise to fame didn't start out easily.

When Steve Young began his career at BYU, he was listed as the eighth quarterback on the team's depth chart. In other words, the coaches considered seven other guys to be better than him. The odds were pretty low that he'd ever play in a game, but he stuck with it and slowly impressed the coaches. Two years later he was named the starting quarterback.

Former BYU coach LaVell Edwards told about that season. Coach Edwards said, "When Steve was a junior and was starting his first season as our quarterback, we had one of the greatest opportunities presented to us in our football program at BYU. We were scheduled to play Herschel Walker and the University of Georgia, the defending national champions. We worked very hard and felt we had a chance to beat them if we played our very best and did not make mistakes.

"Before 82,000 fans, and on a 'rainy day in Georgia,' Steve threw five interceptions in the first half of the game—more than he would normally throw in five games! In spite of the interceptions and two missed field goal attempts, we were still tied 7-7 at halftime.

"Going into the dressing room, I thought to myself that I must talk to Steve and assure him that everything would be fine. The rain, the crowd, the tipped balls—I had all the excuses ready for throwing five interceptions in one half. I started explaining this to Steve and before I could finish, Steve stopped me, looked at me as if I was crazy, and said, 'Hey coach, there's no problem. I can hardly wait to get back out there. We're going to win.'

"I found myself thinking, 'What do you mean there's no problem, you dummy? You've just thrown five interceptions!'

"It's the way he thinks. That's what has made him what he is and enabled him to accomplish what he has done. As you know, this was just the start of a career that would see him become one of the finest quarterbacks to play the game of college football."[1]

Steve Young's greatness comes from his determination to never give up, especially when times are tough. It's a great attribute that we should make a part of our own lives.

Action creates power

It is a true principle that the more we actively seek to do good for others, the more power and confidence we will gain.

Elder Victor L. Brown once told the men of the

Church that he felt we could all do better in our priesthood service. He said, "I desire to give a challenge to every officer of the Church who has an Aaronic Priesthood responsibility. This includes every deacon, teacher, and priest, as well as adult leaders. Let us share a vision of what the Aaronic Priesthood can become and then join together in a great, continuing effort to make that vision a reality.

"If doing the work of the priesthood is the aim of an Aaronic Priesthood quorum, its members will become active and remain active. Members invariably lose interest if the quorum presidency or adult leadership ignores the work of the Lord and attempts to devise entertainment programs to entice activity. It is a law of life: 'Only if you sacrifice for a cause will you love it.'

"Frequently, priests who have been frivolous and immature before their missions rapidly grow up after a few difficult months in the mission field. Testimony, purpose, and peace of mind replace lack of direction, confusion, and apathy. The explanation is simple: they learn to sacrifice for a lofty cause.

"Brethren, Aaronic Priesthood holders should not have to wait for the mission field before experiencing the joy of sacrifice associated with service to God and mankind. They should not have to wait until they reach the age of nineteen before having cause to love and even defend the priesthood."[2]

Defending the truth with an egg basket

Elder Brown's comment about defending the priesthood reminds me of my ancestor Finity Daybell, who took a stand for the truth when he certainly could have walked the other way.

Finity was a member of the Church in England during the 1860s, when Elder Joseph F. Smith was serving a mission there. The missionaries faced a lot of persecution and even death threats, yet they continued preaching the gospel.

One day Elder Smith and his companion were speaking to a crowd in the town square. Soon one of the men in the crowd brought out a basket of rotten eggs. He and his friends began throwing the eggs at the missionaries. Elder Smith was wearing a stovepipe hat, and an egg splattered against it.

At this moment, Finity came into the square. He had come to town to fix his plow, but when he saw what was happening to Elder Smith, he took action. He knew the missionaries had been told not to fight back, but he knew that he certainly could!

Finity ran toward the men throwing the eggs. He grabbed the egg basket from them and swung it forcefully. He didn't hit anyone with his first swing, but the men knew he meant business and quickly scattered as Finity reared back and swung again.

Soon only Finity and the two missionaries stood in the square. Elder Smith stepped forward and thanked Finity for his courage.[3]

Hyrum showed compassion to his brother

You don't have to swing a basket of rotten eggs at people to show your devotion to the Lord. There are other—and more peaceful—ways.

Lucy Mack Smith, the mother of the prophet Joseph Smith, told how her son Hyrum gave valuable service when his younger brother Joseph was ill.

Sister Smith wrote, "Joseph's leg soon began to swell and he continued to suffer the greatest agony for the space of two weeks longer. During this period I carried him much of the time in my arms in order to mitigate his suffering as much as possible; in consequence of which I was taken very ill myself. The anxiety of mind that I experienced, together with physical over-exertion, was too much for my constitution and my nature sank under it.

"Hyrum, who was rather remarkable for his tenderness and sympathy, now desired that he might take my place. As he was a good, trusty boy, we let him do so, and, in order to make the task as easy for him as possible, we laid Joseph upon a low bed and Hyrum sat beside him, almost day and night for some considerable length of time, holding the affected part of his leg in his hands and pressing it between them, so that his afflicted brother might be enabled to endure the pain which was so excruciating that he was scarcely able to bear it."[4]

There are times—as with Finity and Hyrum— when our actions truly speak louder than words.

Service is often never forgotten

You might be surprised at how long a small act of service can carry on. One of the most unexpected experiences I've had in my life began when I did a service project to earn my Star Scout award. It was the week before Christmas, and as I pondered what I could do for the project, I thought of the people in my neighborhood. We were the first young family to move into our neighborhood in many years, so most of our neighbors were elderly couples or widows. I realized I had never given them a Christmas card, so I picked out ten neighbor families and created a homemade card for each of them.

Believe me, these cards were very low-tech—I folded a piece of notebook paper in half, wrote "Merry Christmas" on the front in alternating red and green letters, and then wrote a paragraph or so in each card, complimenting them on what good neighbors they were, and things such as how I appreciated that we could play football in their backyard. I delivered each card on Christmas Eve and I thought that would be the end of it.

Then a strange thing started happening. These people began saying "hello" to me at Church, and I actually became good friends with all of them.

The impact of those cards struck home again last year when I attended the funeral of one of those neighbors—more than twenty years after I gave them the card. The deceased man's widow came up to me and gave me a hug. Then she said, "You know, we still have your homemade Christmas card. That really meant a lot to us."

You can make great things happen when you are a teenager that can bless your entire life. When President Wilford Woodruff was an elderly man, he made this statement to the young men of the Church: "I desire to impress upon you the fact that it does not make any difference whether a man is a priest or an apostle, if he magnifies his calling. A priest holds the keys of the ministering of angels. Never in my life, as an apostle, as a seventy, or as an elder, have I ever had more of the protection of the Lord than while holding the office of a priest. The Lord revealed to me by visions, by revelations, and by the Holy Spirit, many things that lay before me."[5]

That same opportunity awaits you as you magnify your calling in the Aaronic Priesthood.

Chapter Three

Authority
Action
Reverence
Obedience
Nobility
Integrity
Covenants

When I was a teacher, my friend Rob Barrus and I were assigned to take the sacrament to elderly, home-bound people in our ward. Rob would drive us to each house on his motor scooter, and I'd try to stay on the back of the scooter with our ties whipping in the wind. Thankfully, I never fell off, despite Rob jumping off a curb once in a while to see if I could stay on the back.

Rob wasn't necessarily known in our ward as the most reverent person, but when we stepped through the front door of those homes, he would be on his best behavior. Rob, who was a priest, would give the sacrament prayers, and I would pass the bread and water to the people.

We could feel the Spirit in those homes, and much of the Spirit was brought there by our own actions of reverence and quiet politeness. We were often the only contact with the Church those people would have that week, and tears would sometimes come to their eyes as they shared their joy at being able to partake of the sacrament.

We developed a particular friendship with a man named Milt Harrison. Milt was nearly blind and his legs no longer worked, yet he had a wonderful personality. We looked forward to our visit each week with him, because Milt would leave us feeling much better about ourselves than we had when we arrived.

More importantly, we would always feel the Holy Ghost strongly during our visits with Milt. Our surroundings weren't fancy, and the bread and water for the sacrament were simply placed on a stool in the front room, but we knew that our efforts were important to Milt, and to the Lord. Reverence came automatically at those times.

I learned from Rob that there is a time for fun—and Rob certainly knew how to have fun—but he also taught me that there is definitely a time for reverence. As you learn that difference, you will become a powerful servant of the Lord.

Reverence during the sacrament

As my friend Rob demonstrated, one of the most important times for an Aaronic Priesthood holder to show reverence is during the sacrament. The ward members are all watching you and expect you to behave properly.

Elder Dallin H. Oaks, in the October 1998 Priesthood Session of General Conference, gave some wise counsel on this subject. He said, "I will now suggest how teachers and priests and deacons should carry out their sacred responsibilities to act in behalf of the Lord in preparing, administering, and passing the sacrament.

"I will not suggest detailed rules, since the circumstances in various wards and branches in our worldwide Church are so different that a specific rule that seems required in one setting may be inappropriate in another."

Elder Oaks then emphasized, "Deacons, teachers, and priests should always be clean in appearance and reverent in the manner in which they perform their solemn and sacred responsibilities. Teachers' special assignments in preparing the sacrament (prior to the meeting) are the least visible but should still be done with dignity, quietly and reverently. Teachers should always remember that the emblems they are preparing represent the body and blood of our Lord."[1]

In an orderly manner

Elder Oaks explained that our actions as priesthood holders can improve—or hurt—the spirituality of the meeting itself. He said, "Deacons should pass the sacrament in a reverent and orderly manner, with no needless motions or expressions that call attention to themselves. In all their actions they should avoid distracting any member of the congregation from worship and covenant making."

Elder Oaks makes another key suggestion that will help maintain reverence—singing the sacrament hymn! He said, "With the single exception of those priests occupied breaking the bread, all who hold the Aaronic Priesthood should join in singing the sacrament hymn by which we worship and prepare to partake.

"No one needs that spiritual preparation more than the priesthood holders who will officiate in it. My young brethren, it is important that you sing the sacrament hymn. Please do so."[2]

Blessing the sacrament

The first time I blessed the sacrament, I was fairly calm until the moment I knelt down to give the blessing on the bread. Suddenly it felt as if my tongue had expanded in my mouth, and I got a dry twitch in my throat that made me want to cough. I glanced down at my family, and although my parents had their heads bowed, my brothers were watching me very closely, so the pressure was on.

Despite all the obstacles, and a couple of pauses, I made it nearly to the end of the prayer before saying "and keep his commandments which he has given *him . . .*" instead of the word *them.*

I knew I had made an error, but I hurriedly finished the prayer, hoping no one had noticed. I glanced over at the bishop, and he mouthed to me, "Do it again."

It was a bit embarrassing to start over again, but now I am glad the bishop respected the sacrament ordinance itself, and didn't say "Good enough" just so I could avoid embarrassment. I learned a valuable lesson that day.

Elder Oaks made some important observations about how priests should perform the prayers. He said, "To avoid distracting from the sacred occasion, priests should speak the sacrament prayers clearly and distinctly. Prayers that are rattled off swiftly or mumbled inaudibly will not do."

Elder Oaks then shared a painful experience from his own life. He said, "As a 16-year-old priest, I was just beginning a part-time job as a radio announcer at a local station. After I offered a prayer at the sacrament table in our ward, a girl who was present told me I sounded like I was reading a commercial.

"Can you imagine the shame I felt? After fifty years that rebuke still stings. Brethren, remember the significance of those sacred prayers. You are praying as a servant of the Lord in behalf of the entire congregation. Speak to be heard and understood, and say it like you mean it."[3]

A humbling lesson

President Thomas S. Monson told of a similar incident from his Aaronic Priesthood years where a young man showed his true devotion to the Lord.

President Monson said, "I remember as a deacon watching the priests as they would officiate at the sacrament table. One priest had a lovely voice and would read the sacrament prayers with clear diction—as though he were competing in a speech contest. The older members of the ward would compliment him on his 'golden voice.' I think he became a bit proud.

"Another priest in the ward had a hearing impediment which caused his speech to be unnatural in its sound. We deacons would twitter at times when Jack would bless the emblems. How we dared do so is beyond me: Jack had hands like a bear and could have crushed any of us.

"On one occasion Barry with the beautiful voice and Jack with the awkward delivery were assigned together at the sacrament table. The hymn was sung; the two priests broke the bread. Barry knelt to pray, and we closed our eyes. But nothing happened. Soon we deacons opened our eyes to see what was causing the delay.

"I shall ever remember Barry frantically searching the table for the little white card on which were printed the sacrament prayers. It was nowhere to be found. What to do? Barry's face turned pink, then crimson, as the congregation began to look in his direction. Then Jack, with that bear-like hand, reached up and gently tugged Barry back to the bench. He, himself, then knelt on the little stool and began to pray: 'Oh God, the Eternal Father, we ask thee in the name of thy Son, Jesus Christ, to bless and sanctify this bread to the souls of all those who partake of it . . .'

"He continued the prayer, and the bread was then passed. Jack also blessed the water, and it was passed. What respect we deacons gained that day for Jack who, though handicapped in speech, had memorized the sacred prayers. Barry, too, had a new appreciation for Jack. A lasting bond of friendship had been established."[4]

Elder Boyd K. Packer gave this important insight concerning the sacrament. He said, "I have, as a member of the Quorum of the Twelve Apostles, passed the sacrament. I assure you I have felt honored and humbled beyond expression to do what some might consider a routine task."[5]

Show respect while home teaching

Home teaching visits are another time when we should show our best behavior. Home teaching companions come in all shapes and styles. Thankfully, I was companions with one of the best— my neighbor David Prothero. When I turned 14, my father was companions with an elderly man who wanted them to stay together, so from the time I became a teacher until the week I began my mission, David and I were companions. David was known as a faithful hometeacher, and his High Priest group leader assigned him to families that some would call "challenging."

David has always had the ability to make people feel comfortable, even when the people knew we were there to talk about the gospel. Sometimes I wondered if David was *ever* going to talk about the church, but he eventually did, and in a non-threatening way. He showed reverence and respect to our home teaching families—never putting too much pressure on them—but encouraging them to come to church when they felt ready.

One particular widow we visited had a poodle named Fluffy. For some reason that dog and I never got along. Fluffy would spend most of the visit barking and nipping at my feet, and I secretly dreamed of launching Fluffy right out the open window. But David acted like Fluffy wasn't even in the room, devoting all of his attention to the sister. I followed David's example and never hinted to the sister that maybe Fluffy would enjoy time alone in a locked room during our visit.

We also visited a man named Jim. He and David would talk about everything under the sun except the gospel, but he was always friendly to us. As a teenager, I didn't quite understand David's motives.

"Why isn't David telling him not to smoke?" I'd think to myself. Thankfully, David realized that being Jim's friend was more important than anything else at that time.

Interestingly, as circumstances have changed in Jim's life, the gospel has now become important to him. And guess who is right there to help him along? That's right—David.

So make it a goal to be the most polite, patient, and respectful home teacher you can be—even if Fluffy is nipping at your feet.

Show reverence in your daily life

Reverence is essentially showing respect to your Heavenly Father. This should be a part of your daily life. The Holy Ghost will be with you if you seek to have a reverent attitude. Prayer can be a big part of that. In the Book of Mormon we are taught that we should always have a prayer in our hearts.

Amulek taught, "Let your hearts be full, drawn out in prayer unto him continually for your welfare, and also for the welfare of those who are around you." (Alma 34:27)

President John Taylor told of how his experiences with prayer as a young man prepared him to accept the gospel when it was taught to him. He said, "I am reminded of my boyhood. At that early period of my life I learned to approach God. Many a time I have gone into the fields, and, concealing myself behind some bush, would bow before the Lord and call upon him to guide and direct me. And he heard my prayer."6

A towering example

When I was attending BYU, one day I rounded a corner and came face-to-bellybutton with Shawn Bradley. Shawn happened to be the seven-foot six-inch star of the BYU basketball team. I looked up at him and apologized. He smiled down at me and said it was no problem, and I've been looking up to him since—in more ways than one.

Shawn has played for many years in the NBA, including several seasons with both the Philadelphia 76ers and the Dallas Mavericks.

Shawn has attracted national attention for his basketball skills ever since he was in the ninth grade. College recruiters roamed around his hometown of Castle Dale, Utah, trying to persuade Shawn to consider going to their colleges.

But Shawn had one big requirement, and if schools would not agree, then there was no more discussion with them. Shawn told them that as soon as he turned 19 he would be taking two years off to serve a mission. That point was non-negotiable. Shawn finally chose to go to BYU, about a two-hour drive from his home.

Shawn did serve a mission in Australia, but even before that he had opportunities to share the gospel.

When Shawn was 15, he and another LDS player from Utah attended a national basketball camp with 120 of the best high school players in the United States. Shawn made new friends, and one player in particular had some pretty strange ideas about Mormons.

The player asked Shawn, "There are Mormons where you're from, right? Do you see them? Do you live by them?"

Shawn told him, "Yeah, we go to school with them. We see them all the time. Mormons are like you and me. They're normal people. They look like us, dress like us, and act like us. They even talk like us."

The other player didn't believe him, though, until Shawn said, "I can prove to you that Mormons are just normal people."

The young man asked, "How?"

Shawn replied, "My friend and I are both Mormons."

Shawn said it really shook the young man up, but a few days later the player started asking Shawn more about the Church. Shawn said they had a good talk about living the law of chastity and keeping the Word of Wisdom.

"It was a heavy-duty discussion for 15-year-olds," Shawn said, "but I ended up bearing my testimony to him. That is the best missionary tool in the world. I just couldn't find a way of explaining everything I knew. But I knew it was true. It was an excellent feeling to know something is really true." 7

Shawn has remained a strong example of living the gospel to people across the nation. He was recently recognized by a national magazine, *The Sporting News*, as a professional athlete who is "willing to do charity appearances, talk to school kids, make hospital visits—whatever the community asks."8 The teachings he learned as an Aaronic Priesthood holder still carry through in his life today.

Doing our part

Reverence for the gospel means more than just sitting quietly in church with your arms folded. It can become a part of your daily life as you let the Holy Ghost guide you.

We often hear about "having the Holy Ghost with us," but sometimes it isn't clear what exactly people mean when they say that. The influence of the Holy Ghost has been described in many ways—from feeling a warm sensation in your chest to having a thought come into your mind that guides you in a certain way. Such a prompting is often called "hearing the still, small voice." By receiving such promptings, it simply means you are living in such a way that the Lord can help you in your life.

The list on the following page comes from the *Ensign* magazine and gives good guidelines on whether you have the Spirit with you.

When you have the Spirit with you:

- You feel happy and calm. You are glad to be alive.
- You feel filled with light and your mind is clear.
- You feel confident in yourself.
- You don't mind if others see what you are doing.
- You are glad when others succeed.
- You want to make others happy. You bring out the best in others, and respect young women.
- You gladly perform church ordinances, and enjoy attending your Sunday meetings.
- You feel like praying.
- You seek to keep the Lord's commandments.
- You have your emotions under control.
- You seek to have pure thoughts and actions.

When you don't have the Spirit with you:

- You feel unhappy and depressed. You wonder if life is really worth it.
- You feel heavy and dark inside. Your mind is muddled and you feel empty.
- You become easily discouraged.
- You become secretive. You try to avoid others, especially your family.
- You are envious of others' triumphs and their worldly possessions.
- You don't want to pray.

- You are critical of others, especially your family members and authority figures in your life.

- You feel hesitant and unworthy to perform priesthood ordinances.

- You find the commandments to be bothersome, restricting and senseless.

- You have difficulty controlling your temper.

- You let evil thoughts dwell in your mind.9

Naturally, since we all have our shortcomings, we likely have times when feelings found on the second part of the list creep into our lives. However, hopefully you look at that list and feel pretty good about how you are living your life.

If you feel you aren't doing so well, there is always hope. The way is open for us to become like the Savior Jesus Christ, one step at a time.

The Great Physician

President Thomas S. Monson gave this counsel of how to make the Savior a part of our lives. If we let Him, the Savior will spiritually heal us.

President Monson said, "He is the Great Physician—but He is more than a physician. He who rescued the 'lost battalion' of mankind is the literal Savior of the world, the Son of God, the Prince of Peace, the Holy One of Israel—even the risen Lord—who declared, 'I am the first and the last; I am he who liveth, I am he who was slain; I am your advocate with the Father.'"

Then President Monson added, "My dear brethren, let each of us:

- Learn of Him.
- Believe in Him.
- Trust in Him.
- Follow Him.
- Obey Him.

By so doing, we can become like Him."[10]

I know the Savior lives, and He is eager to help each of us return to our heavenly home. Please let Him become a part of your daily life.

Chapter Four

Authority
Action
Reverence
Obedience
Nobility
Integrity
Covenants

Capitol Reef National Park in southern Utah is a spectacular place filled with steep sandstone cliffs, mysterious canyons, and natural stone arches.

My grandfather, Guy Chesnut, grew up in Fruita, Utah, the small town that later became part of Capitol Reef. The actual one-room school house that Grandpa attended as a child is still there for the public to visit.

Our family used to go to Capitol Reef every Memorial Day weekend, and one of my favorite activities was to play in the Fremont River that passes through the park. At one point the river turns into a forty-foot-high waterfall. We would all go there and play beneath the waterfall, and some of the more adventurous relatives would actually stick their heads into the waterfall for a refreshing natural shower.

However, our parents strongly warned us to

never play in the river directly above the waterfall, since someone had actually been swept over the falls and killed a few years earlier.

Well, when I was twelve, my curiosity got the best of me. Without telling anyone, I hiked up the trail above the falls. I looked at the river and couldn't see why my parents were making such a big fuss. The river was only two feet deep and ten feet across, and seemed perfectly safe. The bottom of the river was smooth sandstone, and it was almost like a natural waterslide.

I sat down in the water and let the river slowly push me along. The waterfall was at least fifty yards away, and I was certain I could easily just stand up and get out of the river as I approached it.

Then suddenly the river became much swifter as it approached the waterfall. I quickly stood up, but my feet couldn't grip the sandstone. I slipped onto my stomach twice, and I sensed I was about to get thrown over the waterfall and smashed onto the rocks below. I said a quick prayer, and miraculously this time my feet took hold on the edge of the water- fall. I carefully inched my way to the river bank, and thanked the Lord for saving me.

I must admit my prayer felt a little hollow. I knew that I wouldn't have been in that situation if I had simply obeyed my parents. I'd been warned of the dangers, yet I had ignored them. I quickly learned that obedience is crucial in our daily lives.

What would Jesus do?

Marion G. Romney served in the First Presidency of the Church for many years. When he was twelve years old, Marion received a patriarchal blessing from his grandfather, who placed his hands on Marion's head and told him that if he would be faithful, he would become mighty in expounding the scriptures. He also mentioned other accomplishments Marion could achieve in his life, depending upon his faithfulness to the Church.

The blessing was written down, and from time to time, Marion read it. As he did so, young Marion was filled with a desire to receive those blessings which he said, "helped to keep me in the line of duty."

At about this time, a small pamphlet came into his hands entitled, *"What Would Jesus Do?"* The title remained in his mind all of his life, and it became natural for him to ask himself the question, "What would Jesus do?" and then turn to the scriptures for an answer. He later wrote the following list, which each of us can apply to our own lives.

President Romney said, "The most satisfying solutions to problems—and the best answers to questions—I have arrived at as follows:

"**1.** From my youth I have searched the scriptures.

"**2.** I have tried to honestly face each challenge or question with a sincere desire to solve it as Jesus would solve it.

"**3.** I have, through diligent study and prayer, sought to weigh alternatives in light of what I knew about gospel principles.

"**4.** I have made a decision in my own mind.

"**5.** I have then taken the matter to the Lord, told him the problem, told him that I wanted to do what was right in his view, and asked him to give me peace of mind if I have made the right decision."[1]

The great thing about the process described by President Romney is that we can know for ourselves whether a decision is right. If I had prayed *before* I stepped into the river above the waterfall, I likely would've received an answer that matched my parents' counsel to stay out of the river.

Plan now for an abundant life

We have the opportunity to make decisions as teenagers that can affect our entire lives. President Spencer W. Kimball told the members of the Aaronic Priesthood, "You can determine now that you will be the most faithful deacon and teacher and priest. You can decide that now with an irrevocable covenant. You can be a good student; you can use your time properly and efficiently. All the balance of your life you can be happy if you use your time well.

"You can make up your mind this early that you will fill an honorable mission when you reach mission age, and to that end that you will now earn money and save it and invest it for your mission, that you will study and serve and use every opportunity to properly prepare your mind and heart and soul for that glorious period of your life."2

Make up your mind to be obedient

President Kimball knew the power of obedience from experiences in his own boyhood in Arizona. He said, "I had heard all of my life about the Word of Wisdom and the blessings that could come into my life through living it. I had seen people chewing tobacco, and it was repulsive to me. I had seen men waste much time in 'rolling their own' cigarettes. They would buy a sack of tobacco and then some papers, and then they would stop numerous times in a day to fill the paper with tobacco and then roll it and then bend over the little end of it and smoke it. It seemed foolish to me and seemed such a waste of time and energy.

"Later when the practice became more sophisticated, they bought their cigarettes readymade. I remember how repulsive it was to me when women began to smoke.

"I remember as a boy going to the Fourth of July celebration on the streets of my little town and seeing some of the men as they took part in the horse racing as participator or as gambler, betting on the horses, and I noted that many of them had cigarettes in their lips and bottles in their pockets and some were ugly drunk, with their bleary eyes, coarse talk and cursing.

"It took a little time to match the ponies and arrange the races, and almost invariably during this time there would be someone call out, 'Fight! Fight!' and all the men and boys would gravitate to the fight area which was attended with blows and blood and curses and hatreds.

"Again I was nauseated to think that men would so disgrace themselves, and again I made up my mind that while I would drink the pink lemonade on the Fourth of July and watch the horses run, that I never would drink liquor or swear or curse as did many of these fellows of this little town.

"And so I made up my mind firmly and solidly that I would never touch those harmful things. Having made up my mind fully and unequivocally, I found it not too difficult to keep the promise to myself and to my Heavenly Father."

However, years later there came an opportunity to break his promise. President Kimball said, "I remember once in later years when I was district governor of the Rotary Clubs of Arizona that I went to Nice, France, to the international convention. As a part of that celebration there was a sumptuous banquet for the district governors, and the large building was set for an elegant meal. When we came to our places, I noted that at every place there were seven goblets, along with numerous items of silverware and dishes; and everything was the best that Europe could furnish.

"As the meal got underway, an army of waiters came to wait on us, seven waiters at each place, and they poured wine and liquor. Seven glass goblets were filled at every plate. The drinks were colorful. I was a long way from home; I knew many of the district governors; they knew me. But they probably did not know my religion nor of my stand on the Word of Wisdom.

"At any rate, the evil one seemed to whisper to me, 'This is your chance. You are thousands of miles from home. There is no one here to watch you. No one will ever know if you drink the contents of those goblets. This is your chance!' And then a sweeter spirit seemed to whisper, 'You have a covenant with yourself; you promised yourself you would never do it; and with your Heavenly Father you made a covenant, and you have gone these years without breaking it, and you would be stupid to break this covenant after all these years.'

"Suffice it to say that when I got up from the table an hour later, the seven goblets were still full of colorful material that had been poured into them but never touched an hour earlier."3

An All-American on and off the court

Obedience can bring blessings in every area of your life. A good example of this is former BYU basketball star Devin Durrant. Few BYU basketball players have made an impact on the court like Devin did in the 1980s. If No. 35 shot the ball, the odds were high that the ball was going through the hoop. Devin's scoring ability was well-known, and he was named an All-American his senior year. He then played in the NBA with the Indiana Pacers.

However, his father George Durrant has often said, "I am more proud of the person Devin is off the court than I am of who he is on the court." That is quite a compliment, considering the many records Devin set while playing for BYU.

Brother Durrant told the following story about Devin. He said, "I recall one night at bedtime as Devin was headed for his bedroom we passed in the hall. He extended his hand and said, 'Shake, pops.' I extended my hand. Then without warning, he squeezed my hand to the point where it caused me to cry out in pain, 'Let go.' Regaining my composure, I said in a challenging tone, 'I didn't know you were going to do that. Let's try it again and this time we'll see who's got the strength.'

"He grinned. Our hands met and embraced. As I squeezed with all my strength, pain went throughout my hand. I shouted again, 'Let go!' His grin turned into laughter. After recovering enough to be able to speak, I said, 'So you've got strong hands. Who cares? Strong hands never have proven anything.'

"Then looking at him with soberness, I said, 'All I care about those hands of yours is that they break the bread at the sacrament table, that they never are used to bring any dishonor to yourself or to any young lady, that they hold the holy scriptures, that they fold together in prayer, that the knuckles become raw from knocking on doors while you serve as a missionary, and that they forever remain clean.'

"By now he was no longer grinning. He was always willing to listen to me. The Spirit of the Lord was there and what a thrill it was. We shook hands again and this time there was only a firm grip and a great love between a father and a son."[4]

Why keep a journal?

As a young man, Devin had an interesting hobby that blessed his life. When his older brother was on a mission, he sent a letter to Devin that said, "Devin, you ought to start a journal. The prophet has counseled us to do it. I have been writing regularly in one and it has helped me a great deal. My journal is something that I will treasure forever."

Devin said, "I loved my brother. He was everything that I wanted to be. I thought, 'If he writes in a journal and thinks it's a good thing, then I'm going to do the same.' I turned 16 years old shortly after I received his letter advising me to record the events of my life. For my birthday that year my parents gave me a gift certificate. The following day I went to the store and spent five dollars of that gift certificate to buy my first journal."

Devin continued, "On November 1, 1976, I made

my first entry, and since then every day of my life has been recorded.

"One purpose of my journal is that it serves as a blessing counter. As I write down my experiences, happy and sad, and my feelings about them, I am able to see better the blessings that each day brings. Journal writing is also a valuable teacher for me. It provides a few minutes a night to look on the day and learn from each experience.

"We all need to write in a journal, not only to help ourselves learn and grow and to count our blessings, but to share our experiences with those who follow us in this life."

Devin added, "I surely would like to be able to read about my great-grandfather's first date or his feelings when he was ordained to be an elder. His journal would be a priceless treasure to me.

"I believe my descendants will enjoy reading about my successes and failures and other experiences and feelings that I have had, such as the embarrassment that I felt when the back of my pants ripped out on one of my first dates or the nervousness that ran through my body as I opened the envelope that carried my mission call.

"My journal is a priceless treasure to me. Writing in it has blessed my life. I hope the lives of my descendants will be enriched as they read about my experiences and that they will be inspired to start on their own 'priceless treasure'—a journal."5

Let the Holy Ghost into your life

The reason the prophets encourage us to do things such as read the scriptures and write in our journals is that it helps clear our minds and allows the Holy Ghost to be a part of our lives. The Holy Ghost will prompt us in the right direction.

Your teenage years are filled with excitement and fun, but they also determine your fate for the rest of your life. The Lord is especially concerned with helping you through this time of your life, and if you pay attention, you will receive promptings from the Holy Ghost.

Sadly, sometimes we might receive a prompting and then shake it off. That's what happened to President Wilford Woodruff as a young man, and it was a lesson he never forgot.

He had been visiting in Randolph, Utah, with his family during the holidays when he received this prompting: "Take your team of horses and go home to Salt Lake City."

However, when he told his family about the prompting to leave, they urged him to stay a little longer. He said, "Through their persuasion I stayed until Saturday morning, with the Spirit continually prompting me to go home. I then began to feel ashamed to think that I had not obeyed the whisperings of the Spirit to me before. I took my team and started early on Saturday morning."

When President Woodruff was partway home, he

was overcome by a "furious storm" with powerful winds. President Woodruff said, "In fifteen minutes I could not see any road whatever, and knew not how or where to guide my horses.

"I left my lines loosely on my animals, went inside my wagon, tied down my cover, and committed my life and guidance into the hands of the Lord, trusting to my horses to find the way, as they had twice before passed over that road.

"I prayed to the Lord to forgive my sin in not obeying the voice of the Spirit to me, and implored Him to preserve my life.

"My horses brought me onto the Wasatch station at 9 o'clock in the evening, with the hubs of my wagon dragging in the snow.

"I got my horses under cover and had to remain there until next Monday night, with the snow six feet deep on the level and still snowing.

"It was with great difficulty at last that I saved the lives of my horses by getting them into a box car and taking them to Ogden; while, if I had obeyed the revelation of the Spirit of God to me, I should have traveled to Salt Lake City over a good road without any storm.

"As I have received the good and the evil, the fruits of obedience and disobedience, I think I am justified in exhorting all my young friends to always obey the whisperings of the Spirit of God, and they will always be safe."[6]

Hopefully we can learn from President Woodruff's experience and heed the first prompting of the Holy Ghost, rather than having to be prodded along.

Obedience brings happiness. President Gordon B. Hinckley said, "I give you my testimony that the happiness of the Latter-day Saints, the peace of the Latter-day Saints, the prosperity of the Latter-day Saints, and the eternal salvation and exaltation of this people lie in walking in obedience to the counsels of the priesthood of God."7

Chapter Five

Authority
Action
Reverence
Obedience
Nobility
Integrity
Covenants

You've likely heard your generation described as a "royal generation" and "sons of a noble birthright." What does that mean?

In October 1918, President Joseph F. Smith was in the final days of his life. He had been pondering upon the Savior's death and resurrection, and he was given a vision of the Spirit World. That vision is now known as Doctrine & Covenants Section 138. Verses 53-56 pertain particularly to the young men of today. This is what President Smith said he saw:

"The Prophet Joseph Smith, and my father, Hyrum Smith, Brigham Young, John Taylor, Wilford Woodruff, and other choice spirits who were reserved to come forth in the fulness of times to take part in laying the foundation of the great latter-day work,

"Including the building of the temples and the performance of ordinances therein for the redemption of the dead, who were also in the spirit world.

"I observed that they were also among the noble and great ones who were chosen in the beginning to be rulers in the Church of God.

"Even before they were born, they, with many others, received their first lessons in the world of spirits and were prepared to come forth in the due time of the Lord to labor in his vineyard for the salvation of the souls of men." (D&C 138:53-56)

Much like earthly kings are first trained and prepared as young men, so too are those who hold the priesthood prepared for their earthly missions. You, as an Aaronic Priesthood holder, almost certainly are one of the "noble and great ones" who will help the Lord's kingdom grow and guide others to the true church.

Another powerful scripture tells us of who we really are—Heavenly Father's sons with the potential to become like Him. The prophet Abraham was shown a vision of our life before we came to earth. This vision is found in the Pearl of Great Price. It reads:

"Now the Lord had shown unto me, Abraham, the intelligences that were organized before the world was; and among all these there were many of the noble and great ones;

"And God saw these souls that they were good, and he stood in the midst of them, and he said: These will I make my rulers; for he stood among those that were spirits, and he saw that they were good; and he said unto me: Abraham, thou art one of them; thou wast chosen before thou wast born." (Abraham 3:22-23)

Of course, that doesn't mean life will always be easy. In that same chapter the Lord tells us why we are sent to earth. Abraham 3:25 reads, "And we will prove them herewith, to see if they will do all things whatsoever the Lord their God shall command them."

So yes, life is a test, and even the greatest people who ever lived faced challenges.

Majesty in a jail cell

Perhaps the greatest example of a noble person who endured unjust treatment is the Prophet Joseph Smith. He rarely went more than a few days without enduring some sort of struggle. Yet he endured his challenges, knowing that the Lord was on his side.

The following story about Joseph shows his true greatness. In 1838, Joseph was arrested, once again falsely accused by wicked men. The Prophet and a few of his friends were taken to Richmond, Missouri, where they were jailed awaiting trial.

Parley P. Pratt was one of those with the Prophet. Parley said that one evening the guards were taunting the prisoners by telling of their deeds of murder and robbery among the Latter-day Saints.

Parley knew that the Prophet was awake beside him and was upset by what the guards were saying. Suddenly Joseph stood on his feet and rebuked the guards with great power by saying, "SILENCE, ye fiends of the infernal pit. In the name of Jesus Christ I rebuke you, and command you to be still; I will not live another minute and hear such language. Cease such talk, or you or I will die THIS INSTANT!"

Parley described the moment. He said that Joseph "ceased to speak. He stood erect in terrible majesty. Chained, and without a weapon; calm, unruffled and dignified as an angel, he looked upon the quailing guards, whose weapons were lowered or dropped to the ground; whose knees smote together, and who, shrinking into a corner, or crouching at his feet, begged his pardon, and remained quiet till a change of guards."

Parley then observed, "I have tried to conceive of kings, of royal courts, of thrones and crowns; and of emperors assembled to decide the fate of kingdoms; but dignity and majesty have I seen but once, as it stood in chains, at midnight, in a dungeon in an obscure village of Missouri."[1]

Those of nobility are expected to live a higher standard. Like Joseph, there are certain things you just shouldn't tolerate as a priesthood holder.

Never too young to say "No"

Not long ago my youngest son, Mark, learned to talk. He is a very active child, able to sprint away from us in a grocery store in a split second. He is also an expert climber, and we'll often find him climbing along the top of furniture or in cupboards that he knows he shouldn't be in. Naturally, a word Mark hears quite often is "No."

Unfortunately, that word is now one of his favorite things to say to *us*. One evening after the children had gone to bed, Mark decided he would rather stay up. He came into the living room, and I told him, "Mark, you need to go get back in bed." Instead, he started marching around in a circle, singing "No" over and over.

His singing attracted the attention of the whole family, and soon everyone in the family was out of their beds. We gathered around this cute little boy, and he finally stopped saying "No" as I grabbed him and we all gave him a big hug.

I hope Mark has that same enthusiasm about saying "No" as he gets older. I don't expect him to march around school shouting "No" when he is first offered alcohol, but I do pray that "No" is the word that comes out of his mouth. I would also hope that "No" is a part of *your* vocabulary.

The story of Paul

Recently a man named Paul started attending our Elders Quorum. Paul's fun personality could get the whole quorum in a good mood, but little did we know Paul was struggling against some long odds. One Sunday he told us his story.

Paul had grown up in an LDS family just a block from their church building. He had been a wonderful Boy Scout, and had earned his Eagle Scout Award before he was 14 years old. Then Paul told us, "At that point I made a big mistake. The same month I got my Eagle Scout Award, I took drugs for the first time. It started as a dare from one of the older guys in the neighborhood, but I was hooked from that very first time. My life would be so much different if I had just said 'No.'"

By the time Paul was 18, he had been in jail a few times and his family had spent thousands of dollars to pay for his drug rehabilitation costs. Paul had a hard time finding a good job, and also had a hard time staying away from drugs.

Finally at age 27 he had straightened out his life enough that the Church became important to him, and that is how he had made his way to our quorum. As he finished his story, Paul recited for us the twelve points of the Scout Law. Despite his troubles, he could still remember it after all these years. With tears in his eyes, he told us, "I wish with all my heart I had followed it."

Then last year as our ward Christmas party was ending, an ambulance raced up the street. It stopped at Paul's home. He had suffered a brain aneurysm directly related to his years of drug use. He died two days later.

At Paul's funeral, I hugged his parents and we

talked about what a good, kind person he was. We mentioned how hard he had been trying the past few months to do what was right. But I think we all had the same sad question in our minds: *What if Paul had just said 'No' those many years earlier?*

Although Paul had been taught true principles as a young man, he had forgotten who he truly was— a son of God with a noble birthright as a priesthood holder in the Savior's church. *You* are, too. Please keep that in mind as temptations come your way.

Today's choices affect your future

Elder Robert D. Hales of the Quorum of the Twelve Apostles said, "The choices you make today will directly influence the number and kinds of opportunities you will have in the future. Each daily decision will either limit or broaden your opportunities. As you make righteous decisions during this preparatory period, you will be ready to make righteous decisions in the future.

"Just think, in the next decade of your life—the decade of your 20s—what decisions will be made: temple worthiness, missionary service, education, career, an eternal companion, and a family. This decade of decision is not a time to fear. It is a time to enjoy the blessings for which you have prepared. 'If ye are prepared ye shall not fear.' (D&C 38:20) One of the greatest gifts you were given at baptism was to receive the gift of the Holy Ghost. With the gift of the

Holy Ghost, you can have inspired guidance to make these important decisions."

Elder Hales concluded by saying, "During the preparatory period of your lives it is so important that you cultivate spiritual growth, physical growth, education, personal development, career preparation, citizenship, and social skills. These qualities are all part of your priesthood duties and will help in the decisions that lie ahead for the next decades of your life."[2]

There are many things that you can happily say "No" to, even if what you are invited to do isn't necessarily breaking a commandment. I expect you have more common sense than I did in the following story.

A bad decision

When I was twelve, a family of teenaged boys moved into our neighborhood. Evel Knievel, the daredevil motorcyclist, was popular across the nation, and these boys idolized him. They would build big wooden ramps and jump their bikes over anything they could. One day they built a ramp big enough to jump their bikes over a Volkswagen Bug. I was pretty impressed!

I would watch them each afternoon, but they usually ignored me. Then one day the oldest boy stopped his bike in front of me and said, "Do you want to do something really cool?"

I said "Sure!" I followed him down the street to

his house. When we got there, he said to me, "Lay down on the sidewalk and I'll jump my bike over you." It seemed pretty harmless, so I chose a spot about five feet away from the bike ramp.

He yelled at me, "No, that's too close. Move a little farther." He kept coaxing me until I was about ten feet from the ramp.

In my mind the Holy Ghost was practically shouting at me, "Go home now!" but I ignored the prompting, not wanting to offend this older boy who was suddenly treating me like a friend.

Well, a few seconds later he came pedaling hard down the sidewalk, and at the last moment I started rolling toward the ramp. He flew through the air, and his back tire landed right where my head had been a moment earlier. He skidded to a stop and shouted, "Hey, idiot! Why did you move?" I quickly realized he wasn't my friend at all.

He *was* right about one thing, though. I was being an idiot. Was I breaking a commandment? No. Was I making a bad decision? Yes. The Lord expects us to use common sense in our daily lives, and to heed the promptings of the Holy Ghost.

Peer pressure is real, but the next time you're being pressured to do something that doesn't feel right, picture me foolishly lying on the sidewalk with that bike barreling down on me. Then ask yourself, "Do I really want a tire mark across my forehead?" Then you'll smile and make the right choice.

Live the standards of the Church

As you make wise decisions each day, you will find yourself growing spiritually. President Gordon B. Hinckley said, "Now, my dear young brethren, if we are to enjoy the ministering of angels, if we are to teach the gospel of repentance, if we are to baptize by immersion for the remission of sins, if we are to administer to the membership of the Church the emblems of the sacrifice of our Lord, then we must be worthy to do so.

"You cannot consistently go serve on the Sabbath and fail to live the standards of the Church during the week. It is totally wrong for you to take the name of the Lord in vain and indulge in filthy and unseemly talk at school or at work, and then kneel at the sacrament table on Sunday. You cannot drink beer or partake of illegal drugs and be worthy of the ministering of angels. You cannot be immoral in talk or in practice and expect the Lord to honor your service in teaching repentance or baptizing for the remission of sins. As those holding His holy priesthood, you must be worthy fellow servants.

"I would not wish to leave the impression that these abhorrent practices are common among the young men of the Church, but I know that they are not entirely absent. Most of you are trying to do the right thing, and I compliment you most warmly. But if there be any here who are not doing the right thing, then I plead with you, and I invoke upon you the spirit of repentance, the keys of which you hold as those endowed with the Aaronic Priesthood. Make yourselves worthy in every respect, and the Lord will bless you. You will have peace in your hearts and a greater sense of the remarkable power which has been given to you."3

Never forget that you are part of a noble, royal generation. The Lord is eager to bless you and has great blessings waiting for you if you obey his commandments. I know you have the strength to do what is right!

Chapter Six

Authority
Action
Reverence
Obedience
Nobility
Integrity
Covenants

Dale Murphy recently retired from the major leagues, and he is possibly the best-known LDS baseball player in the world. He was a star outfielder for the Atlanta Braves during the 1980s and 1990s, and he was named the National League's Most Valuable Player in 1982 and 1983, becoming the youngest player to ever to win that award two years in a row.

National sportswriters could hardly believe he was for real. Here was a ballplayer who didn't act like a typical star athlete. Dale's example let many people across the nation know that members of the LDS Church don't drink alcohol, smoke, chew tobacco or swear. His pleasant personality and his eagerness to sign autographs were a welcome relief to fans who were tired of athletes who felt they were better than everyone else.

However, Dale's story might never have taken

place without the example and integrity of a player Dale met in the minor leagues—Barry Bonnell.

A valuable card

I used to collect baseball cards, and I particularly liked to collect rookie cards—cards produced during a player's first season. One of my favorite rookie cards is the 1978 Topps card of Atlanta Braves rookie Barry Bonnell.

Some rookie cards are worth a lot of money, but Barry's is worth about seventeen cents. So why do I find it to be so special? Because Barry performed a feat that has affected the entire Church—he introduced the gospel to Dale Murphy, and later baptized him.

Dale and Barry were teammates on the Atlanta Braves' minor league team in Greenwood, South Carolina. Barry asked some questions about the importance of baptism and eternal life—things Dale knew little about. "We had many long discussions and then got together with the missionaries," Dale said. "And after receiving the lessons, I knew I wanted to be part of it. Barry baptized me after the 1975 season."[1]

Barry went on to have a good professional career, but during the 1978 season Barry had an experience that he described as "life changing." He was struggling terribly, batting about .200. He was down on himself and felt miserable. He really didn't want to go when Dale asked him to join him on a hospital

Braves

BARRY BONNELL

visit, but he went anyway. There he and Dale met Ricky Little, a young Atlanta Braves fan who had leukemia. It was readily apparent that Ricky was near death. Barry felt a deep desire to think of something comforting to say, but nothing seemed adequate.

Finally, Barry asked if there were anything they could do. The youngster hesitated and then asked if they would each hit a home run for him during the next game.

Barry said later, "That request wasn't such a hard thing for Dale, who in fact hit two homers that night, but I was struggling at the plate and hadn't hit a homer all year. Then I felt a warm feeling come over me and I told Ricky to count on it."

That night, Barry hit his only home run of the season.[2]

You don't have to convert a future major-league star or hit a home run to fulfill your duties. If you say you'll collect fast offerings or help with a service project, you'll do it. That's what integrity is all about.

Face the consequences

Before one Scout campout, our Scoutmaster asked us to make a tin foil dinner for ourselves to cook in the campfire. My mom reminded me to make the dinner, and then she ran an errand before I left for the campout.

Our troop had eaten tin foil dinners on the previous campout, and I decided I'd had enough of potatoes, carrots and hamburger. So while Mom was gone, I looked in the freezer and spotted what I thought would be a great tin foil dinner—a frozen pizza. I got out the tin foil and wrapped that frozen pizza up nice, then I stuck it in my backpack just before Mom arrived home. I kissed her good-bye and headed out on the campout.

That night, my pizza was a big hit. Even my Scoutmaster was amazed at my meal. Yes, it did burn a little on the edges, but it really was pretty good. I even chiseled off a few pieces for the other Scouts.

However, I had a nagging feeling this wasn't quite the meal Mom expected me to make. When I returned home the next day, she asked, "Chad, do you know what happened to the frozen pizza that was in the freezer? We were going to have it for dinner tonight, and now it's gone."

It was a time of decision. I'd been gone for a whole day—certainly one of my younger brothers could shoulder the blame. But, somewhat embarrassed, I explained what I had done. She laughed, but wasn't as impressed by my "pizza dinner" as my fellow Scouts had been. However, she thanked me for telling the truth.

In that incident, I can't claim to have displayed complete integrity. I did admit to Mom what I had done, though. The point is that after making a mistake, we need to face up to it. We tell the truth. That is integrity—telling the truth and honoring promises no matter the consequences. The Lord expects us to do so.

Correct your mistakes quickly

Integrity is an especially important quality to have when you are in a position of leadership, such as in a quorum presidency.

When I was serving as the president of our deacons quorum, a young man named Mike had graduated from Primary and was joining our quorum.

Mike's family had been through some rough times, but lately they had started coming to church, and everyone in the ward was happy to see Mike progressing in the gospel.

As part of Mike's first day in our quorum, the bishop came in and ordained Mike to the Aaronic Priesthood. During the ordination, the bishop pronounced Mike's middle name in a way that struck me funny, and I laughed a little. Then the deacon next to me laughed, too, and we struggled to control our giggles.

My giggles stopped immediately, though, when Mike peeked over at me. There was a hurt look in his eyes, and when the ordination ended, the adult leaders didn't look too happy, either.

I looked away and acted like nothing had happened. At the very least, I should have told Mike I was sorry. Then the lesson started, and I hoped everyone would forget about my laughter.

The next Sunday arrived, and Mike didn't come to Church. I felt a little guilty, knowing I was likely part of the reason. His mother and sister still came to church, but Mike *never* came to our priesthood quorum again.

I cringe to think of what he must have told his family after church that first Sunday. He probably said, "They laughed during my ordination. Who needs friends like that? I'm never going again."

I knew I had made a mistake, and the right thing to do—as president of the quorum—would have been to go to Mike's house and apologize as soon as possible. But I never did. Mike moved two years later, and I lost track of what he was doing, although I knew his sister had been married in the temple.

Then in our late teens I crossed paths with Mike again on a summer work project. He seemed happy to see me and we talked like old friends throughout the afternoon. However, I noticed that his hat had the word "Budweiser" across the front, and it was clear in other ways that the gospel wasn't a part of Mike's life.

It is really sad that Mike's deacons quorum president—me—didn't do a better job. I expect to someday answer to the Lord for the role I played— or failed to play—in Mike's life. I hope that in the future Mike will somehow return to the church— probably through a faithful home teacher.

Even if that does happen, Mike has already lost

many years of church activity. If you have a similar situation in your quorum, don't fail to fulfill your duty to be a friend and an example. I know from personal experience the painful consequences that can come if you don't do so.

President Thomas S. Monson has told the young men of the Church, "You can make a difference. Whom the Lord calls, the Lord qualifies. This promise extends not only to missionaries, but also to home teachers, quorum leaders, presidents of branches, and bishops of wards. When we qualify ourselves by our worthiness, when we strive with faith to fulfill the duties appointed to us, when we seek the inspiration of the Almighty in the performance of our responsibilities, we can achieve the miraculous."3

Making commitments to the Lord

President Gordon B. Hinckley recently told of a group of Aaronic Priesthood holders from nineteen stakes in northern California who signed a proclamation to live the gospel. The young men made the following promises:

"We pledge to become converted to the gospel of Jesus Christ. We will study the scriptures. We will pray for strength to obey. We will work. We will strive with all our hearts to follow the example of Jesus.

"We will magnify the priesthood we have been given by serving other people. We will keep

ourselves worthy to administer the sacrament of the Lord's supper. Wherever there is a need for help, like our forefathers, we will step forward.

"We will prove ourselves worthy of the greater, Melchizedek Priesthood. We commit ourselves to the Lord's army and will go forth as full-time missionaries to invite all to come unto Christ.

"We are young men of the covenant. We will prepare ourselves to receive the covenant of eternal marriage. We pray for righteous wives and children whom we will honor and protect with our own lives.

"Be it known that whatever the risks, whatever the temptations, whatever the state of the world around us, as our forefathers were faithful, so we will be. Like those who have gone before, we will turn away from self-aggrandizement and set aside personal gain in order to build a peaceful society, governed by God.

"At all times and in all places, we will be true to our pledge."

After mentioning this proclamation, President Hinckley said, "I compliment every boy who signed this pledge. I pray that not one will ever default on the promises he has made to himself, to the Church, and to the Lord.

"What a different world this would be if every young man could and would sign such a statement of promise. There would be no lives wasted with drugs. There would be no gangs with children killing children and young men headed either for prison or death. Education would become a prize worth working for. Service in the Church would become an opportunity to be cherished.

"There would be greater peace and love in the homes of the people. There would be no viewing of pornography, no reading of sleazy literature. You would honor and respect the girls with whom you associate, and they would never have any fear about being alone with you in any set of circumstances. It would be as if the stripling warriors of Helaman had recruited the youth of the world to their way of living."4

Integrity is vital to our salvation

President Marion G. Romney spoke often of the importance of integrity in our lives. He said it is always required, no matter where we are. To illustrate this point, he told the following story:

"Four Latter-day Saint boys set out from a Utah city on a cross-country trip. They had saved all their money during the last year of high school for this purpose, and now that graduation was over, they packed their suitcases into the trunk of their car and said good-byes to worrying parents and envious friends. It was a matter of considerable celebration when they crossed the Utah state line and entered into another state. They pulled up alongside the highway and got out to see how it felt to be in new surroundings. A certain thrill of excitement was noted by each of the young travelers and a sense of adventure led them to great expectations.

"They had agreed to send their parents a postcard every other day to indicate their whereabouts, and had promised to call if they ran into any trouble. One of the boys commented that it felt real good to be on his own and not be under the necessity of getting advance approval from someone for every move he made.

"Another suggested that they must act like seasoned travelers and not impress others as country boys on their first trip away from home. As a follow-up, this same boy proposed to his friends that they forget all about being Mormons for the duration of their adventure. Asked why by the other three puzzled boys, he said that they could now afford to 'let their hair down' and sample some of the excitement enjoyed by other people, not of the Mormon Church. 'Anyway,' he argued, 'what difference will it make? Nobody out here in the world knows us or cares anything about our church connections.'

"The thrill of the new experience weighted their judgment, and the group made an agreement to give it a try. They decided to announce themselves to the world as students from the East who had been to school in Utah for a short time. Their Utah license plates made this necessary.

"Nightfall on the first day of the journey found

them at a famous tourist attraction spot, and they made arrangements for camping near the resort. After the evening meal they gathered at the large hotel for the night's entertainment. No sooner had they arrived when the ringleader of the boys suggested that they begin here and now sampling the things they had so long been denied by strict parents and teachers.

"The first thing that caught their eyes was a large neon sign at the far end of the lounge. It read, *'Bar—beer, cocktails.'* Thinking it a moderate nod in the direction of 'sinning just a little bit,' they agreed to go into the bar and order a glass of beer for each one. There was a nervous air about them as they entered the gaudily lighted bar and surveyed the counters loaded with intriguing bottles of liquor. The boy who had been delegated to give the order lost his voice on the first try and had to swallow hard to get out an understandable, 'Four glasses of beer, please.'

"What the beer lacked in palatability, the atmosphere and thrill more than made up. They grew bolder and began to talk of the next adventure they would undertake. The talk was growing racy when suddenly a well-dressed man entered the bar and walked straight toward their table. The look on the stranger's face and the determined pace at which he walked toward them left the boys completely unnerved.

"When the man reached the table at which the boys were sitting, he extended his hand to one of them and said, 'I beg your pardon, but aren't you George Redford's son from Utah?' The boy was speechless and terrified. His fingers froze around the base of the glass of beer and he answered in a wavering voice, 'Why, yes, sir, I am.'

"The man replied, 'I thought I recognized you when you came in the lobby of the hotel. I am Henry Paulsen, vice-president of the company your dad works for, and I met you and your mother last winter at a company dinner at the Hotel Utah. I have never forgotten how you explained your Mormon priest-hood to one of the other executives of our company who asked you what it meant to be a Mormon boy. I must say I was a little surprised to see you head for the bar, but I suppose that with Mormons as well as non-Mormons, boys will be boys when they're off the roost.'

"These boys had heard a sermon they would never hear duplicated from the pulpit. They were sick, ashamed, and crestfallen. As they left their half-filled glasses and walked out through the hotel lobby, they had the feeling that everyone was looking at them. The cover of darkness was kind as they made their way to their camp.

"'You just can't win,' said the boy who had proposed their dropping their true identity, trying to ease the tension. 'I'm not so sure,' replied the boy to whom the stranger had spoken. 'If we have any sense left, we can make this experience into the most winning lesson of our lives.'"5

Train your mind

The key to integrity begins deep inside yourself. We have often been counseled to watch our *thoughts*, our *words*, and our *deeds*. It is nearly impossible to commit sins if we don't allow such thoughts to dwell in our minds.

President Hinckley tells an interesting story from when he was assisting President David O. McKay. He said, "I remember going to President McKay years ago to plead the cause of a missionary who had become involved in serious sin. I said to President McKay, 'He did it on impulse.'

"The President said to me: 'His mind was dwelling on these things before he transgressed. The thought was the father to the deed. There would not have been that impulse if he had previously controlled his thoughts.'"6

Seek for integrity in your life, and you'll discover it will only bring you happiness.

Authority
Action
Reverence
Obedience
Nobility
Integrity

Covenants

When I was 16, our stake held a summer youth conference at Snow College in Ephraim, Utah. We stayed in the student dormitories, and that is where I first met a young man who had just moved to Springville. He was a soft-spoken 15 year old, but what I noticed was that he was already 6'2" and weighed 250 pounds. His name was Eli Herring.

During high school I watched Eli develop into an All-State football player, helping our team go undefeated and win a state championship in 1985. Eli stood out in other ways, too. He remained that soft-spoken young man I had first met years earlier, and there was little doubt about his firm testimony of the gospel. He was a strong example to everyone, and could be counted on to obey the commandments and to keep the Sabbath day holy.

Fast forward a few years to 1994 when Eli was a senior at BYU. He had served a successful mission, gotten married, and had been an All-Conference offensive lineman for the Cougars during his junior season. Professional teams were beginning to show a real interest in him.

Eli realized that he had a good chance at a career playing in the NFL. He thought about how much he would enjoy it and how much money he could make, but he also realized that as a professional football player, he would have to play football on Sunday. This caused Eli serious concern as he wondered whether that would be the right decision.

Eli knew he could do good things with the money he could earn as a professional football player. He could pay his children's college and mission expenses and he could go on missions with his wife. Essentially, he could do whatever he wanted after his football career was over without worrying about money.

As Eli struggled to make his decision, he remembered reading about Erroll Bennett. When Erroll joined the Church, he decided to stop playing soccer on Sunday, even though he was a top soccer star in Tahiti and not playing on Sunday would mean he would have to quit his team.

Eli was very impressed by Erroll's courage. Eli said, "I knew I wanted to be a man like that, with that kind of commitment and dedication to what I knew was right."

Eli's parents and wife said they would support

him in whatever he decided. Eli fasted and prayed, and he also carefully read the scriptures. It took him six months to come to a final decision.

Ultimately Eli decided that for him, keeping the Sabbath day holy was more important than playing professional football and making lots of money.

"I read my scriptures, and time after time I would see more and more reasons that I felt in my heart that I needed to observe the Sabbath more than I needed to play football," Eli said.

When the 1995 NFL Draft came around, the Oakland Raiders drafted Eli in the sixth round, even though they knew of his decision. The team hoped to change his mind, but he turned down their offer and now teaches and coaches at a high school. He does not make a lot of money, but he is happy.

Eli said, "The paychecks now, in spite of being low, are more than we were making when we were students. We're happy to have more than we had before. Occasionally I think we could have a brand-new car or a nice house, but I have never had any serious doubts about the decision."[1]

The overall purpose of the Aaronic Priesthood is to teach us to make commitments—or covenants— with Heavenly Father and prepare us for the rest of our lives.

Eli's experiences as an Aaronic Priesthood holder and the covenants he honored each week guided his decision.

I like this summary by President Thomas S. Monson. He said the Aaronic Priesthood's purpose is to help each young man grow by:

1. *Becoming converted to the gospel of Jesus Christ.*
2. *Magnifying his priesthood calling.*
3. *Giving meaningful service.*
4. *Being prepared to receive the Melchizedek Priesthood.*
5. *Committing to serve a full-time mission.*
6. *Living worthy to receive the temple covenants and preparing to become a worthy husband and father.[2]*

We achieve those goals a step at a time, with the key being that we continue to make right choices.

Be faithful, and opportunities will come

Eighth grade wasn't my favorite year. In many ways, it was a struggle—my body decided not to grow that year, making me one of the shortest guys in school. Then some of my friends found new ones, and other friends started going a bit off the right path. At school I wasn't necessarily unpopular, yet I wasn't popular, either. I was just kind of *there.*

A few days before Thanksgiving a group of boys I didn't know very well invited me to meet them after school. I did, hoping to make some new friends. I met them down by the creek that ran through our town, and I was surprised to see one of the boys holding a six-pack of beer. He offered me one, but instead I just said "No thanks" and turned toward home as they laughed and yelled rude things at me.

As luck would have it, the guy who had invited me to join them, a boy named Matt, was assigned to sit next to me in woodshop class when the new term started. From then on, he would punch me in the shoulder whenever the teacher wasn't looking and would call me vulgar names. I should have told the teacher, but I figured it would only lead to me getting slugged after school rather than in class.

Let's just say I was relieved when summer finally came, and I was dreading ninth grade. I prayed for a better experience during the coming school year.

By the first day of ninth grade I was feeling a little better about myself. I had grown four inches over the summer—and I wasn't registered for woodshop.

Toward the end of our gym class, a tall boy with dark hair came into the room and talked with the coach. It took me a second, then I recognized him as my distant relative Les Chappell. We had only met once before, at a family reunion earlier that year. He had just moved to our town from Texas.

Soon the coach told us to go to the locker room so we could be assigned our gym lockers. Everyone else ignored Les, and I started moving to the locker room too, but then I looked back. Les was just standing there, looking lost and nervous. Then came a pivotal moment in my life. I felt prompted to turn back and introduce myself to him.

I stuck out my hand and said, "Hi there. I think we're cousins."

Les' face quickly changed to a big smile as he said, "You're Chad, right?" He was very glad to see me, and we hit it off right away. It felt like I'd been reunited with a long-lost friend.

We got our lockers next to each other, and found we had a common interest in sports. I also discovered something else—Les was a talented basketball player. He made our junior high team, and quickly became well-known for his three-point shots. Through Les, I got to know some other wonderful young men that I wouldn't have become friends with otherwise. We helped each other stay on the right path, and we are all still close friends today.

I sometimes shudder to think what my life might have been like if I hadn't heeded the prompting to turn back and introduce myself to Les, especially when I heard his side of the story. He later told me that he had been praying even before he had left Texas that he could find a friend who wanted to live the gospel. I was essentially praying for the same thing, and the Lord answered both of our prayers.

As a holder of the Aaronic Priesthood, you are privileged to receive similar promptings. Maybe your first day of ninth grade won't be the turning point of your life, but who knows? If you honor your priesthood and stay in tune with the Holy Ghost, the Lord can open doors that will bless your life.

An interesting sidenote to this story came when I was in the Missionary Training Center at the start of my mission. One day I heard a voice call out, "Chad!" I turned around and saw Matt, my eighth grade bully. He had moved away after tenth grade, and I hadn't seen him since. I had grown to 6'2" by then and he was now several inches shorter than me.

As much as I wanted to slug him hard in the arm, I could only laugh inside as he talked about the "good times" we'd had in woodshop. I was pleased to see that he had changed his ways and was going on a mission.

We talked for a few minutes, and then we parted with a handshake and a smile. So it was fun to see that my former bully had cleaned up his act—and that I was now bigger than him.

Matt, wherever you are, all is forgiven!

Repentance is possible

That brings up a good question, though. What if *you* are currently the bully at school? Or possibly you have another problem that is dragging you down spiritually. Is it possible to change your ways? Yes! It will take some work, but believe me, if Matt could make the change, you certainly can.

Elder Dallin H. Oaks said, "Young men, if any of you are unworthy, talk to your bishop without delay. Obtain his direction on what you should do to qualify yourself to participate in your priesthood duties worthily and appropriately."3

One step at a time

As we have mentioned, the Lord expects you to advance through the priesthood. As you do so, you will receive assignments and make promises—or covenants—to serve the Lord.

Doctrine & Covenants Section 20 was given to Joseph Smith as he was preparing to establish the LDS Church in 1830. In this revelation the Lord makes it clear what he expects from his priesthood holders. This section also includes the baptismal prayer and the sacrament prayers. I encourage you to read this section as soon as possible to better understand your own duties. We will summarize them here briefly.

The **deacon** is to watch over the church as a standing minister, and to assist other priesthood members as called upon. (D&C 20:57-59)

The **teacher** is to "watch over the church always, and be with and strengthen them." (D&C 20:53) This would include your home teaching assignments.

The **priest** is to "preach, teach, expound, exhort, and baptize, and administer the sacrament, and visit the house of each member." This includes home teaching as well as collecting fast offerings in areas where that takes place door-to-door. The teachers and deacons can assist with fast offerings as well. (D&C 20:46-47)

Such service will prepare you to become a missionary. There isn't anything more important you can do at age nineteen than serve a full-time mission. The good you will do as a servant of Jesus Christ will bless the rest of your life and carry on into eternity.

Elder Joe J. Christensen of the First Quorum of the Seventy said, "The Lord did not say, 'Go on a mission if it fits your schedule, or if you happen to feel like it, or if it doesn't interfere with your scholarship, your romance, or your educational plans.' Preaching the gospel is a commandment and not merely a suggestion. It is a blessing and a privilege. Remember, the Lord and his prophets are counting on you."[4]

Climb all the way to the top

As you advance through the Aaronic Priesthood, it is like climbing a mountain. At the top of the summit awaits your ordination to the Melchizedek Priesthood.

When I was fourteen, our ward's young men decided to climb Mount Timpanogos, the mountain that towers above the Provo-Orem area. Since it was summer, we decided to start hiking at 10 p.m. and pace ourselves so we would arrive at the peak just as the sun was coming up in the east.

I hiked along pretty well for the first couple of hours, but then I reached Emerald Lake, where the ground levels off temporarily. There is also a concrete building near the lake where people can take shelter.

When I reached the concrete building, it was well after midnight. I had developed a bad headache and my legs were feeling tired, so I told myself I'd just take a rest. Another boy, Mickey, was feeling the same way, so our leaders agreed that we could rest for a few minutes and then catch up.

Well, the next thing I remember was a beam of sunlight hitting me in the face. I had slept the rest of the night on that concrete floor! I never got to see the sunrise, or beautiful Utah Valley below. I was disappointed with myself then, and even more now, because I have yet to attempt that hike again.

I suppose I could blame my leaders for leaving me behind (they showed up soon afterward), but there is a good comparison to my experience on the mountain and how some of our young men progress in the priesthood.

Church statistics show that many boys start the hike (become deacons) and a great many of those boys make it to Emerald Lake (become a teacher or even a priest) but not nearly enough young men are making it to the top of the mountain and receiving the Melchizedek Priesthood.

I encourage you, even if you start to feel a little tired on this journey, to keep pushing to the summit. When you make it to the top, it will be well worth the effort. In this case, it will lead you to eternal life. And while you're on your way to the top, please check that concrete building as you pass by. There's probably someone in there who needs to wake up. They might be a little grumpy with you at first, but someday they'll greatly appreciate that you helped them to the summit.

You can truly make a difference in the lives of family and friends. President Gordon B. Hinckley has taught, "We are a covenant people, and great are the obligations which go with that covenant. We cannot be ordinary people. We must rise above the crowd. We must stand a little taller. We must be a little better, a little kinder, a little more generous, a little more courteous, a little more thoughtful, a little more outreaching to others."5

I salute you for making it to the end of this book, and also for your diligence in living the gospel. May the Lord bless you as you advance through the Aaronic Priesthood—on your way to eternal life.

Notes

Chapter 1 — Authority

1. Hinckley, Gordon B. "The Aaronic Priesthood—A Gift from God," *Ensign,* May 1988, p. 44.
2. Skousen, W. Cleon. *The Third Thousand Years,* Bookcraft, 1964, p. 404-405.
3. Packer, Boyd K. "The Aaronic Priesthood," *Ensign,* Nov. 1981, p. 30.
4. Ibid.
5. Woodruff, Wilford. *Leaves from My Journal,* Salt Lake City: Juvenile Instructor Office, 1882, p. 8.
6. Ibid., p. 16-18.
7. Packer, Boyd K. "The Aaronic Priesthood," *Ensign,* Nov. 1981, p. 30.

Chapter 2 — Action

1. Edwards, LaVell R. "Prepare for a Mission," *Ensign,* Nov. 1984, p. 44.
2. Brown, Victor L. "The Vision of the Aaronic Priesthood," *Ensign,* Nov. 1975, p. 66.
3. Brickey, Eva Daybell. *The Life of Finity and Mary Daybell,* unpublished manuscript in possession of the author, p. 5.
4. Smith, Lucy Mack. History of Joseph Smith by His Mother, Lucy Mack Smith. Edited by Preston Nibley. Salt Lake City: Bookcraft, 1954. p. 54-55.
5. Woodruff, Wilford. *Millennial Star,* 5 Oct. 1891, p. 629.

Chapter 3 — Reverence

1. Oaks, Dallin H. "The Aaronic Priesthood and the Sacrament," *Ensign,* Nov. 1998, p. 37.
2. Ibid.
3. Ibid.
4. Monson, Thomas S. "The Aaronic Priesthood Pathway," *Ensign,* Nov. 1984, p. 41.

5. Packer, Boyd K. "The Aaronic Priesthood," *Ensign,* Nov. 1981, p. 30.
6. *Journal of Discourses*, vol. 22, Oct. 19, 1881, p. 314-315.
7. Thomas, Janet. "Someone to Look Up To," *New Era*, Dec. 1990, p. 26.
8. "Willing, Ready and Able," *The Sporting News*, , July 7, 2003, p.14.
9. *Ensign*, August 1978, p. 33.
10. Monson, Thomas S. "Today Determines Tomorrow," *Ensign,* Nov. 1998, p. 48.

Chapter 4 — Obedience
1. Howard, F. Burton. *Marion G. Romney: His Life and Faith.* Salt Lake City, Utah: Bookcraft, 1988, p. 35.
2. Kimball, Spencer W. "Planning for a Full and Abundant Life," *Ensign,* May 1974, p. 86.
3. Ibid.
4. Durrant, George D. "Just Be My Son," *New Era*, Nov. 1980, p.7.
5. Durrant, Devin. "The Blessing Counter," *New Era*, Nov. 1981, p. 42.
6. Hartshorn, Leon R., *Classic Stories from the Lives of our Prophets*, Deseret Book, 1981, pp. 115-116.
7. Hinckley, Gordon B. "If Ye Be Willing and Obedient," *Ensign*, Dec. 1971, p. 125.

Chapter 5 — Nobility
1. *Autobiography of Parley P. Pratt*, p. 211.
2. Hales, Robert D. "Fulfilling Our Duty to God," *Ensign,* Nov. 2001, p. 38.
3. Hinckley, Gordon B. "The Aaronic Priesthood—a Gift from God," *Ensign,* May 1988, p. 44.

Chapter 6 — Integrity
1. Wolsey, Heber G. "Dale Murphy-MVP," *Ensign,* Apr. 1985, p. 58.
2. Monson, Thomas S. "Precious Children: A Gift from God," *Ensign,* Nov. 1991, p. 67.
3. Monson, Thomas S. "You Make a Difference," *Ensign,* May 1988, p. 41.

4. Hinckley, Gordon B. Hinckley. "To the Boys and to the Men," *Ensign,* Nov. 1998, p. 51.

5. Romney, Marion G. Romney, "Integrity," *Ensign,* Nov. 1974, p. 73.

6. Hinckley, Gordon B. "Be Ye Clean," *Ensign*, May 1996, p. 48.

Chapter 7 — Covenants

1. Richardson, Joseph. "To Keep It Holy," *New Era*, Oct. 1997, p. 34-37.

2. Monson, Thomas S. "Today Determines Tomorrow," *Ensign,* Nov. 1998, p. 48.

3. Oaks, Dallin H. "The Aaronic Priesthood and the Sacrament," *Ensign,* Nov. 1998, p. 37.

4. Christensen, Joe J. "The Savior Is Counting on You," *Ensign,* Nov. 1996, p. 41.

5. Hinckley, Gordon B. *Teachings of Gordon B. Hinckley,* Deseret Book, 1997, p. 149.

About the Author

Chad Daybell lives in Springville, Utah, with his wife, Tammy, and their five children. This is his tenth book.

The idea to write *The Aaronic Priesthood* began during Chad's years of working with youth as a Scoutmaster and a Young Men's advisor. The final inspiration for the book, however, came during his calling as the second counselor in the Stake Young Men's Presidency.

Each month he would visit with and teach the Aaronic Priesthood members throughout the stake. This book emerged as a way to help guide these young men to live the gospel seven days a week, rather than just on Sunday.

To learn more about Chad and the other books he has written, please visit **www.cdaybell.com**.

About the Illustrator

Rhett E. Murray received a bachelor's degree from Southern Utah University in Fine Art, and a master's degree from Southern Utah University in Art Education. He also completed a bachelor's degree in fine arts from the Northwest College of Art in Seattle, Washington.

He grew up in Springville, Utah, and served for two years in the Chile Osorno Mission. He lives in Las Vegas, Nevada, with his wife Holly, and their three children. He has taught middle school and high school for the past ten years in Alaska, Washington and Nevada.

He is a member of the Nevada Art Guild, and is also a professional portrait artist and illustrator. He also illustrates Chad and Tammy Daybell's *Tiny Talks* series.

Other books by Chad Daybell

The Youth of Zion
This non-fiction book is filled with inspiring stories and quotes from the modern prophets, and gives guidance on thirty timely topics facing today's families.

The Tiny Talks series
Written with Chad's wife Tammy, this highly popular series has helped thousands of families and teachers with Primary and Family Home Evening lessons.

The Emma Trilogy
This award-winning LDS series includes the novels *An Errand for Emma*, *Doug's Dilemma*, and *Escape to Zion.* The novels are exciting time-travel adventures that teach the three missions of the church.

Chasing Paradise
Chad's newest novel is a captivating journey that takes place on both sides of the veil as Tina Marlar seeks to reunite her family for eternity.

One Foot in the Grave
A humorous collection of strange-but-true stories that occurred while Chad was employed as a cemetery sexton.

Visit **www.cdaybell.com** to learn more about these titles and upcoming books.